Starting
Crocodile

Claire Llewellyn
illustrated by
Simon Mendez

Mangrove trees

Dragonfly

Crocodiles lay their eggs in t dry season when the water in the swamp is low. In the wet season, heavy rain could flood the nests.

The crocodile does not lie on her eggs to keep them warm. The sun's heat will do this for her.

Eggs

Water lettuce

It is a warm, dry evening in the mangrove swamp. A crocodile is high on a bank making her nest. She scrapes the earth with her short, strong legs to make a hole. In it, she lays a clutch of eggs and covers them with leaves and mud.

Once the eggs are buried, the female makes a burrow in the muddy banks nearby. There she guards the nest from predators.

The female lays 20 to 50 creamy-white eggs. They have hard, tough shells.

Damselfly

3

Crested caracaras sweep over the swamp, hunting for small turtles, water snakes, fish, and frogs.

Crested caracara

Crow

Yolk

The embryo will spend three months inside the egg before it is ready to hatch.

Embryo

Hidden inside their underground nest, the eggs begin to change. Inside each egg an embryo develops, taking nutrients from the rich yellow yolk.

Crocodile eggs are tempting meals for raccoons, birds, and rats—but few predators get past the female crocodile.

Raccoon

Earwig

The temperature in the nest is very important. If the temperature is very high in the first few weeks of development, then more of the crocodiles will be male.

Live oak

Egg tooth

Teal ducks live on the sheltered water. They feed by tipping their bodies over and straining food from the water.

Teal

After three months, the mud covering the nest has baked rock-hard in the sun.

Every hatchling has a small bump on its snout called an egg tooth, which it uses to break the shell. After hatching, the "tooth" drops off.

Three months after the eggs were laid, the embryos are fully developed. They are called hatchlings now. From her burrow, the female crocodile hears the hatchlings grunting. This is the sign that they are ready to hatch. Quickly, she opens up the nest to let the hatchlings out.

Hatchling

Sometimes the crocodile gives her hatchlings a helping hand by rolling the eggs inside her mouth until she feels them crack.

Mangrove swamps
create a sheltered
habitat. They grow
near the coast,
protecting the land
from the wind
and waves.

Black-necked stilt

Hatchlings

Reeds and rushes grow
thickly in the water.
They will help to hide the
hatchlings and keep them safe.

The new hatchlings hurry down to the water. Some crawl while others ride in their mother's jaws. They look just like their mother except that they are only 10 inches (25 cm) long! Their dry, scaly skin is greenish-brown, with darker bands and blotches on their backs and tails.

Green heron

The baby crocodiles are an easy catch. A green heron grabs one with its beak.

The hatchlings follow their mother down to the water. She will protect them from predators.

Mosquitoes

Female crocodile

For a few weeks, the female crocodile protects the pod. She rescues any hatchlings that wander away and guides them back to the reeds.

Mosquitoes start life as larvae in the water. After one week, the larvae change into adults and take to the air.

Sedges and rushes

Mosquito fish

Tiny mosquito fish feed on mosquito larvae.

The young hatchlings stay together in a group called a pod. They hide from danger in the rushes and reeds. This is where they learn to snap up water bugs, dragonflies, frogs, and fish with their sharp, little teeth. If one of the hatchlings strays away from the pod, it may be attacked by a male crocodile or another swamp animal. Lost hatchlings call loudly to their mother, and she guides them back to the pod.

Red-eared turtle

Mangrove roots

Not many trees can grow in swamps. Mangrove trees have roots like stilts to support them in the soft, squishy mud.

The young crocodiles grow fast and they are soon fierce and strong. By their second year, they are about 2½ feet (76 cm) long. They are called juveniles now and are no longer in danger from the adult males or any other creature in the swamp. With their bigger teeth and stronger jaws, they can attack water birds, rats, and larger fish. Each day the crocodiles leave the water to warm themselves in the sun.

Juvenile

Dragonflies patrol the swamp, hunting for tiny insects. Their wings reflect the sunlight as they fly.

Juveniles grow 10 inches (25 cm) bigger every year. The skin on their backs gets darker, and any markings begin to fade.

Giant water bug

The skin is thick, tough, and scaly. It protects the animal like a coat of armor.

Adult male crocodile

An adult male crocodile is one of the largest reptiles in the world.

Rat

A crocodile becomes an adult when it is 8-10 years old. An adult male is a huge creature and measures up to 19 feet (6 m) long. Its skin is an olive-gray color and covered in tough, bony scales, except on the belly where it is pale and smooth. Crocodiles and alligators are often confused, but it is easy to tell them apart. A crocodile's snout is narrower and more pointed, and if you look closely when its mouth is closed, you can see a tooth on its lower jaw. On alligators, this tooth cannot be seen.

Snout

Fourth tooth

When the crocodile's jaws are closed the lower teeth are hidden except for one. The fourth tooth can be seen fitting neatly into a groove on the upper jaw.

Water moccasin

Water moccasin snakes are found in and near the water. They are fierce hunters of fish and frogs, and will also eat any baby crocodiles that have been abandoned.

Swamp rabbit

Spicebush swallowtail

Crocodiles always live near water—in slow-moving, freshwater rivers and lakes, or salty creeks and swamps. Some kinds even live in the sea. All crocodiles are expert swimmers. They use their powerful tails to drive themselves forward, and their feet to slow down or turn.

Bass

Crocodiles swim by beating their tails against the water—first one way and then the other.

Webbed feet help the crocodile to swim. On land, they stop it from sinking on soft, muddy ground.

Crocodiles can stay underwater for up to an hour. They don't drown because they have flaps in their throat that stop water from entering their lungs. Other flaps seal their nostrils, eyes, and ears, making them fully waterproof!

A crocodile's eyes, ears, and nostrils are all on top of its head. It can lie very low in the water and still breathe, smell, see, and hear.

Longnose gar

Tarpon

Crocodiles have an extra pair of see-through eyelids. These protect the eyes and help the animals see while they are under water.

Stinkpot turtle

Crayfish

Water snail

17

It is evening and a crocodile slips into the water. It is time to catch a meal. The animal lies so low and keeps so still that water birds, crabs, turtles, fish, and snakes don't even know it is there. Then suddenly— SPLASH!—it lunges forward and grabs one in its jaws.

The crocodile keeps very still until the perfect moment to strike. When it lies low in the water, it could be mistaken for a log because its skin looks just like tree bark.

Sudden bursts of speed and power make crocodiles dangerous hunters. They attack birds that come to feed in the water.

The strong jaws can crush a turtle's shell, but they are no good at cutting or chewing. The crocodile must either tear its catch into bite-sized pieces, or swallow its meal whole.

Sharp teeth

Crocodiles have 66 sharp, pointed teeth. If they lose one while hunting, it will grow back eventually. Each tooth can be replaced 45 times!

Roseate spoonbill

Gray plover

Flocks of birds wade through the water, searching for shellfish, shrimp, and fish. A roseate spoonbill feeds by sweeping its head from side to side in the water. Any creatures that bump into its bill are instantly snapped up.

Crocodiles belong to a group of animals called reptiles. Reptiles are animals with scaly skin, and most of them lay eggs on dry land.

Brown pelican

Brown pelicans are expert fishers. They have a baggy pouch under their bill, which they use to scoop up fish.

Crocodiles do not like the cold. They are only found in the tropics where the weather is always warm.

Crocodiles often lie in the sun with their mouths open. This is called gaping. It allows heat to escape and helps to keep them cool.

Reptiles are cold-blooded animals. This means that their body temperature changes with the temperature outside. After the cool night crocodiles are sluggish, so they bask in the morning sun. Slowly their body temperature starts to rise, and they become more active. Later, when they get too hot, the crocodiles cool off in the river or a shady burrow.

Plover

Some birds, such as the plover, peck insects from the crocodiles' skin. This helps keep them free of parasites, so the crocodiles do not attack the birds.

In the breeding season, the males try to drive one another away. They raise their snouts, slap their jaws, and thrash their tails in the water.

During courtship, the male crocodiles call to the females using a low grumble or growl.

The year passes, and the breeding season comes around again. The male crocodiles court the females. Soon they pair off together. One month after mating, the females lay their eggs, and once again new crocodiles are starting life.

Male crocodile

River otter

River otters eat whatever is easiest to catch. They will be a danger to the new crocodile hatchlings.

Female crocodile

The male crocodile has glands under his jaw that produce a smelly substance called musk. The male rubs the musk over the female to encourage her to mate.

Glossary and Index